I0617210

50+ Color Pages

Easy HALLOWEEN HACKS

for Busy Moms

AJ KIKUMOTO

Visit us at
www.AJKikumoto.com and www.QueenPublishingAgency.com

Welcome to an excellent resource for Easy Halloween Hacks for Busy Moms!
Use knives, scissors, and sharp objects described in this book carefully with adult supervision.
The author is not liable for any accident or misuse of such items. Be careful with permanent markers, such as black Sharpies, as they stain.

Text and Illustrations copyright © 2022 by Yellow Daisy Publishing

All rights reserved. No part of this book may be reproduced or transmitted in any form or by any means, electronic or mechanical, including photocopying, recording, or by any information storage and retrieval system, without permission from the publisher. For information, address Yellow Daisy Publishing at aj.yellowdaisypub@gmail.com

ISBN: 978-1-953556-16-5

www.QueenPublishingAgency.com

SPOOKTACULAR TABLE OF CONTENTS

Best Hacks

INTRODUCTION

Introduction

Welcome to the best resource for some quick, easy tips for costumes, food, class parties, and crafts for one, if not the best holiday, **HALLOWEEN!**

We have six kids, so all holidays are a blast, but Halloween is our favorite! Fall leaves, change of temperature, fall foods, and of course, the costumes!!!!

Some years we go all out, and other times we make it simple and enjoy our time together. Whatever season it is for you and your family, enjoy!

Remember, there is no right or wrong answer. You don't have to do all the fabulous ideas we have compiled in this book. Just pick the ones that work for you in this season of your life and most of all, **ENJOY YOUR FAMILY TIME!!!!**

Now just a quick side note. Your definition of easy and my definition of easy might be two different things. Please share some grace if you think something in this book is difficult. We might have different opinions on the definition of "easy," but please enjoy what we compiled for you.

Now flip through the book, grab an idea or three, and **DO IT!** Please report to us how things went and any additional ideas you have for a potential sequel. The creators are documented in the Resources section at the end of this book.

Please follow us on our **Social Media Handles** and send us some love:

Facebook:
Amy Jo Loveland Kikumoto
Zoey's Great Adventures
Queen Publishing Agency

Instagram:
@ajkikumoto
@zoeysgreatadventures1
@queenpublishingagency

Happy Howling Halloween!!
The Kiks Krew

Top 10

Chapter One
CLAIRVOYANT COSTUMES

Easy Costumes For Busy Moms

1. Witch

Grab a witch's hat and wear all black

2. T-shirt Momma

Wear your Favorite Halloween T-shirt and jeans.

3. Pumpkin Momma

Materials:
Orange T-shirt
Black fabric pens
Directions:
1. Grab an orange T-shirt. Lay flat on a solid surface.
2. Draw a pumpkin face with your black fabric pen

EASY FAMILY COSTUMES

4. Frankenstein Family Costume For the Win

Materials:
Box or brown bag for each person
Black sharpie marker
Scissors

Directions:
1. Cut the bottom and top off each box or brown bag

2. Cut out eyes: First measure by putting the box/bag on and seeing where your eyes are. Cut 2 medium size circles so you can see out.

3. Draw and Color! Draw your monster face. Add hair and Eyebrows. Scars. Nose. Mouth.

4. Wear black, brown and/or tan colors. Jeans are great. Add a jacket or coat if it is snowing.

5. Walk like a monster and moan and groan for special effects.

Dollar Store Finds

Don't have a lot to spend?

It's time to run to the local Dollar Store! You might be surprised by what great finds you will discover!

Let us know what finds you discover!

Some of our finds:

5. Pretty Princess

Pink boa

Sparkly wand

Crown

Face sticker gems/makeup

Wear your favorite dress. Add accessories. Remember your bucket to collect candy!

6. Kitty Kat

Headband, tail, and bowtie.

Wear all black. Use a black face crayon and draw a kitty nose and whiskers

7. Ladybug

Ladybug Wings, Polka dot skirt, Ladybug headband with antennae

8. Miscellaneous Accessories

Super Hero Capes, sparkly boas, witch's hats, masks, helmets, mermaid pieces, unicorn pieces, police accessories, etc.! Dress up an all-black outfit or jeans with affordable accessories.

9. Ghouly Ghosts

White bed sheet
Black Sunglasses

Cut out holes so you can see (ASK mom FIRST!!)

Wear sunglasses over the holes.

Moan like a ghost, and have fun!

10. Pumpkin Head

Use a real pumpkin for the best effect, but a faux pumpkin is more comfortable.

Carve out the eyes and nose, and mouth of the pumpkin.

Cut the bottom of the pumpkin and gut.

Wear jeans, a flannel shirt, and your cool pumpkin head! As pictured, a skirt/dress with black fishnets is excellent too! Have FUN!!

Top
16

Chapter
Two

FABULOUS
FOOD

1. Super Easy Healthy-ish Pumpkin Chocolate Cookies

Ingredients:
1 can pumpkin (100% pure pumpkin, 15 oz)

1 box Spice cake mix (don't follow the directions, literally just the cake mix)

1 (or ½ bag, 10 oz) chocolate chips. I like the minis. Ghirardelli's is our family favorite.

Directions:
1. Mix cake mix and pumpkin together. A hand mixer helps. Add chocolate chips. For a healthier option, only use half a bag of chocolate chips. Use a cookie dough scoop and drop balls onto a cookie sheet.
2. Bake 350°, 8-10 minutes, golden brown on the bottom.
3. Voila! Enjoy

2. EASY HOMEMADE ROOTBEER

Ingredients:

1 bottle root beer extract
4 lbs sugar
5 gallons water
7 lbs dry ice

Directions:

1. Mix all the ingredients.
2. Add the dry ice. Be very careful with dry ice. Avoid burns and use gloves.

3. EASY ROASTED PUMPKIN SEEDS

1. Scoop out the seeds from a pumpkin
2. Wash and lay the seeds flat to dry. Dry overnight is best.
3. Put 1 TBSP olive oil in a Ziploc baggie. Add the dry seeds. Seal the bag and have the kids shake the bag to coat the seeds.
4. Lay the seeds flat on the cookie sheet.   Sprinkle with a dash of salt.
5. Bake at 250° For 20 minutes or until golden.

4. EASY NO BAKE CHOCOLATE PEANUT BUTTER BALLS

Ingredients:

½ cup softened butter

1 ½ cups peanut butter

2 ½ cups powdered sugar

1 package of chocolate chips, plain M&M s, Hershey's kisses, or white marshmallows)

Directions:

1. Mix butter, peanut butter, chocolate chips orM&Ms, and powdered sugar until well blended.
2. Chill in the refrigerator for 10-15 minutes.
3. Roll into 1-inch balls.
4. Place on a cookie sheet with parchment paper.
5. Freeze in the freezer for 20 minutes until firm.

OPTIONAL

Melt Ghiradelli® chocolate chips in a microwave-safe bowl. Follow the directions on the back of the package.

Dip the peanut butter balls into the chocolate.

Add candy eyes for Halloween/Fall/Monster effect.

Add Hershey's Kiss, marshmallow, or colored M&M in the center

6. Optional: Press the balls down with a fork. Crisscross.

5. OREO COOKIE DESSERT

Ingredients

1 ¼ lb package Oreo cookies, crush, set aside ¼ cup

1 stick butter - softened

1 large container of Cool Whip

8 oz. cream cheese

1 large package of instant chocolate pudding

2 ½ cup milk

Directions:

1st Layer – Mix the crushed Oreo cookies with the butter. Press in a 9x13 pan

2nd Layer – Mix ½ the container of cool whip with softened cream cheese.

Spread mixture on top of the crust.

3rd Layer – Mix instant chocolate pudding with milk – spread on top

4th Layer – Top with the remaining cool whip & sprinkle with crushed Oreos

Refrigerate. Chill 20 minutes before serving.

Cut in squares to serve.

7. EASY HOMEMADE CARAMELS

**requires an electric frying pan

Ingredients:

2 Cups Sugar

1 ⅓ cups Light Karo corn syrup

3 Cups Whipping Cream

(Found By the milk section at the grocery store.

HALF pint= 1 cup (school milk size))

1 ¼ tsp vanilla extract

Chopped walnuts

Directions:

1. Combine sugar, syrup, and 1 cup of cream in the electric frying pan
2. Set the electric frying pan to 325°
3. Stir. Not fast or hard.
4. when the light goes off, Add 1 cup of cream.
5. when the light goes off, add 1 cup of cream.
6. When the light goes off, add vanilla, then walnuts.
7. Pam spray 9x13 pan. Pour. Let set.
8. Cut into 1-inch squares or rectangles.
9. Wrap squares/rectangles in Saran wrap.

7. EASY HOMEMADE VANILLA ICE CREAM

Ingredients:

4 cups half-and-half or light cream

1 (14 oz) can sweeten condensed milk

2 TBSP vanilla extract

Directions:

1. Combine all ingredients in a large bowl.
2. Mix well
3. Pour into a freezer-safe container
4. Freeze until firm, about 4-6 hours

TRY THIS: add some fruit, sliced bananas, sliced strawberries, raspberries, blueberries, sliced peaches, cinnamon, chocolate chips, cookie dough, etc.

Makes 12 servings

8. Five Minute Ice Cream

Ingredients:

Frozen fruit puree

Heavy cream

Food processor or blender

Directions:

1. Slowly pour the cream over the pureed frozen fruit in a blender or food processor.

2. The frozen fruit quickly freezes the cream and makes instant ice cream!

9. Ice Cream Topping

Ingredients:

2 – 6 oz. Cans Red Hawaiian frozen punch

1 – 6 oz. Can frozen orange juice

1 small can of crushed pineapple

10 bananas, sliced

Directions:

1. Mix the frozen punch and frozen orange juice together.
2. About 1 hour before serving, add about ten bananas (sliced).

Serves about 20.

Put a scoop of topping in the dish and then the vanilla ice cream. Add another scoop of topping for a beautiful effect.

10. MOMMA'S BEST SUGAR COOKIES

Ingredients:

2 Cups Butter

3 Cups Sugar

4 Eggs

4 tsp Grated Orange Peel / 4 drops orange oil

4 tsp Vanilla extract

¾ Cup Milk

8-9 Cup Flour

1 tsp Salt

2 tsp Baking Powder

2 tsp Baking Soda

Directions:

1. Heat oven to 350º
2. Cream butter and sugar
3. Add eggs
4. Add orange peel (optional orange oil)
5. Mix in vanilla and milk
6. Combine dry ingredients: Flour, salt, Baking Powder, and Baking Soda. Add to the cookie dough mix
7. Roll out on a floured surface. Cut out fun Halloween shapes. OR just simple circles using the top of a glass.
8. Bake at 350º for about 8 minutes or until golden on the bottom. Do not overbake.
9. Frost!   See the Easy Buttercream Frosting recipe. OR use your favorite canned frosting if in a pinch.
10. Enjoy! Take to school parties. Have the kids frost. OR drop off at the neighbors'!

11. EASY BUTTERCREAM FROSTING

Ingredients:
3 cups powdered sugar
1 cup Butter softened (2 sticks)
3 TBSP milk
1 ½ tsp vanilla
pinch salt

Directions:
Mix all ingredients well. If the frosting seems too thick, add milk. If the frosting seems too liquid, add more powdered sugar.

12. THE BEST CHOCOLATE CHIP COOKIES IN THE WEST

Makes approximately 50 small cookies. We always double this recipe.

Ingredients:

1 cup butter (or butter flavor shortening)

¾ cup sugar

¾ cup brown sugar (firmly packed)

1 tsp vanilla extract

½ tsp water

2 eggs

3 cups flour

1 tsp baking soda

1 tsp salt

Directions:

1. Cream butter and sugars.
2. Add vanilla, water, and eggs.
3. Beat well
4. Mix flour, soda, and salt in a separate bowl.
5. Add the flour mixture to the butter mixture.
6. Mix slowly so the flour doesn't go everywhere
7. Add 2 cups chocolate chips (Ghiradelli milk or semi-sweet chocolate chips are our favorites) and mix.
8. Scoop in 1-inch balls onto a cookie sheet. Use parchment paper or silicone baking sheet covers for easy clean-up.
9. Bake 350° for 8-10 minutes. Bottoms should be golden brown

Variations:

1. Add 1 cup of nuts (chopped walnuts)
2. Add 4 cups Rice Krispies or Corn Flakes cereal (grind in the blender for a different texture)
3. 2 Cups chopped dates
4. 1 TBSP grated orange peel
5. 2 cups raisins
6. 1 cup peanut butter

**Double the recipe for double the goodness to share with neighbors/friends

13. BLOODY FINGERS

Ingredients:

Hot dogs
Ketchup
Hot dog Buns

Directions:

1. Adults: Take a small paring knife, carve out a fingernail, and 3 lines like finger joints
2. Adults: grill hot dogs on a grill until browned
3. Kids: spread ketchup all over the inside of a hotdog bun with the back of a spoon
4. Place the hotdog finger in the bun and serve.

14. POTATO MONSTERS

Ingredients:

Small gold potatoes
Paring knife

Directions:

1. Adult: cut out faces and pieces of the potato to look like a face.
2. Triangle eyes. Triangle teeth. Triangle nose. Keep it simple and fun.
3. Place cutout potatoes in a baking dish. Bake at 350º degrees for approximately 45 minutes until golden brown. Drizzle with olive oil and sprinkle with salt if desired.

15. VAMPIRE DONUTS

Ingredients:

2 dozen sprinkle donuts
2 dozen vampire fangs plastic teeth
2 dozen sets of candy eyes.
Fake edible blood-red frosting

Directions:

Buy sprinkle donuts – at the nearest grocery store or donut place. 2. Flip the donut upside down. 3. Insert fake vampire teeth. 4. Insert fake candy eyes. 5. Add some blood with edible blood-red frosting.

16. CARAMEL APPLES

Ingredients:

Green apples (Granny Smith)
Caramel wraps
Popsicle Sticks
Red ribbon

Directions:

1. Insert a wooden popsicle stick into the bottom of the apple. Hint: Sometimes, I have had to insert a knife first to get the popsicle stick in the apple. (Adults only with sharp knives). Skewers work well.

2. Wrap the apple with the caramel wraps. (Backup. If you can't find the caramel wraps: Unwrap and melt the caramels in a microwave-safe bowl. Then dip apples into the caramel)

3. Place on wax paper Options: Dip tops into melted chocolate. Add nuts. Add sprinkles. Add mini marshmallows.

Top 10

Chapter Three

DECADENT DECORATIONS

1. HALLOWEEN SKULLS/ SKELETONS

Materials:

Dollar Store skull
Any other materials you have

Directions:

Decorate your skull to your liking!

Options: spray glue on the skull, and cover it with gold glitter.

Gotta a wig?

Sunglasses?

Hat?

These are some fun ways to decorate a skull or skeleton.

Be creative and have FUN!

2. JAR OF EYEBALLS

Materials:

Ping pong eyeballs or chocolate eyeballs
Empty glass jar

Directions:

Fill the empty jar with eyeballs.

Add Halloween ribbon, jute, or hot glue a plastic skull to the lid.

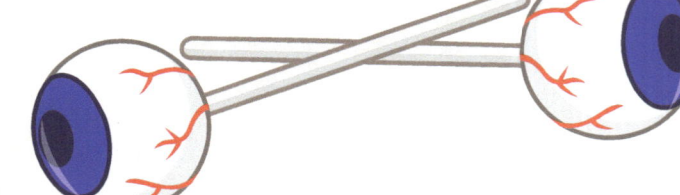

3. PAPER BATS

Materials:

Black and white construction paper

Scissors

Directions:

Cut out bat shapes from black construction paper or black card stock.

Place them on the wall by the fireplace like they are flying out of the fireplace.

4. GIANT SPIDER DECOR

Materials:

Large foam craft balls
Black paint
Paintbrush
Black pipe cleaners (8 per ball/spider)

Directions:

Paint the large foam craft balls black.

Wait for them to dry.

Poke the pipe cleaners into the foam ball, like spider legs. (8 legs per spider)

Voila! Giant spiders you can place on your porch or around the house. A sure hit!

5. GHOST BALLOONS

Materials:

White balloons
Black Sharpie marker
White crepe paper.

Directions:

1. Draw eyes and a mouth with the Black Sharpie on the balloon.
2. Blow up white balloons, and tie the knot.
3. Add white crepe paper to dangle from the bottom of the balloons.

6. MONSTER WREATH

Materials:

2 orange feather boas

Wiggly eyes in different sizes and shapes

Glue gun

Wire or plastic wreath (craft shop)

Directions:

1. Glue the orange boas onto the bare wreath.
2. Glue on the wiggly eyes randomly around the wreath.

7. WIGGLY EYES GOURDON

Materials:

Wiggly eyes, different sizes

Gourds of all shapes and sizes

Glue Gun or Elmers Glue

Directions:

Glue on wiggly eyes onto an "ugly" gourd. Use Elmer's Glue if you are with kids.

8. PUMPKIN. PUMPKIN

Materials:

Lots and lots of pumpkins. Different sizes, colors, shapes, and styles. Bumpy, smooth

Directions:

Place pumpkins all along your porch, front entrance, driveway, etc.

Pumpkins are great for Halloween, fall decor, and the next holiday, Thanksgiving. "Kill two birds with one stone," as the saying goes, and decorate for both holidays.

9. SMOKIN PUMPKIN

Materials:

1 real pumpkin, gutted and carved
Fog machine

Directions:

Place the fog machine inside or behind the pumpkin.

Watch all the neighbors and children squeal with joy.

TIP: If you don't have a fog machine, grab one the day after Halloween for a screaming deal for next year!

10. GOBBLE GOBBLE PUMPKIN

Materials:

1 large pumpkin
1 small pumpkin

Directions:

1. Gut and carve out a large pumpkin
2. Use a scallop knife to cut eyes, nose, and mouth for a unique look
3. Add the small pumpkin inside the large pumpkin mouth.

OPTION. Use the guts and seeds as part of the decor like the pumpkin is spitting out his guts.

Top 12

Chapter Four

CLEVER CLASSROOM PARTIES

1. Build Your Own Monster

Materials:

1 oz molding clay or play dough (different colors)

3-5 Different size wiggly eyes

4-6 Pipe cleaners, cut in half

4-6 Pom poms, different colors, sizes, shapes

Directions:

Be creative!

Stick on whatever parts you want to create your very own monster!

Option: Put individual materials into a Ziploc baggie. Write each student's name on the baggie.

2. Trick-or-S'more Treat

Ingredients:

Hershey's mini chocolate bar

Peeps Ghost-colored marshmallows, or plain white marshmallows

Graham cracker squares

Directions:

Build your own S'more!

Cracker, chocolate, marshmallow, cracker.

Think outside the box and be creative.

3. Glow Your Night with a Little Light

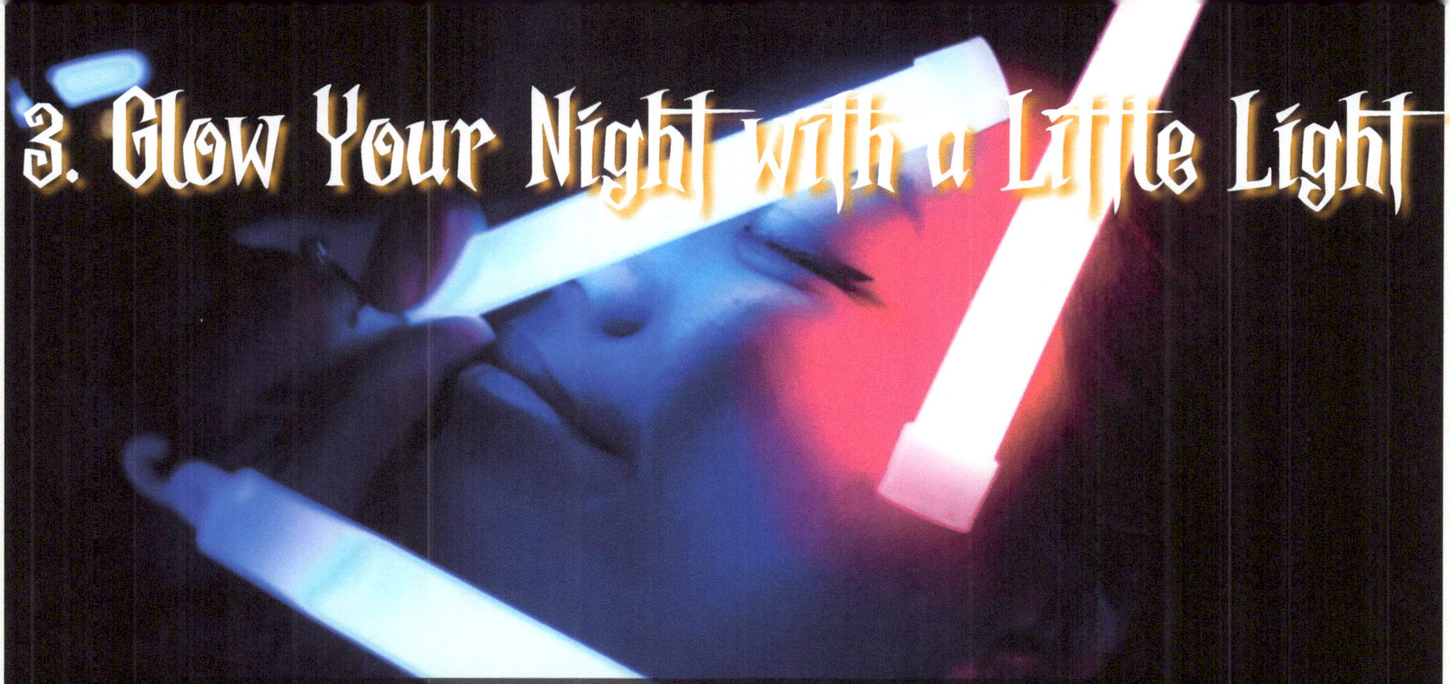

This is a great handout for the classroom and Halloween night.

Materials:

Glow Sticks!

Print up cute labels with this saying and tape them on the glow sticks.

All the parents will thank you for keeping their child safe with a glow stick while trick or treating.

4. Kisses and Bugs

Materials:

Hershey's silver kisses
Fake plastic bugs/spiders
Ziploc Baggie

Directions:

Place a handful of chocolate kisses and plastic bugs/spiders (spider rings) into a clear baggie.

Print a cute label (or handwrite in scary letters) that says Kisses and Bugs.

33

Minute-to-Win-It Games

These fun games can be set up in a classroom, your home, or your backyard. Adjust times and distances to be age appropriate.

Most importantly, Have FUN!!!!

5. Popcorn Pumpkin Shuffle

Materials:

2 plastic pumpkin buckets.

A huge bag of popcorn (Costco has a huge bag of SkinnyPop).

Directions:

Set the timer for 1-3 minutes (age appropriate). Kids stand in equal file lines. Start the race. The team that transfers the most popcorn from bucket to bucket wins.

6. Pumpkin Mini Golf

Materials:

Pumpkin with mouth open (optional: an orange cup, laid down on its side)
Golf balls.
Golf Putter.

Directions:

Use the golf putter to put golf balls into the pumpkin (or cup). Start farther away for older kids. Set the timer for 1-2 minutes, depending on the age.

Goal: Most balls that make it into the pumpkin win.

7. Easy Homemade Bubble Solution

1. Combine 1/2 cup water, 2 TBSP dish soap, and 2 tsp. salad oil or glycerin.

2. Mix thoroughly.

3. Dip the bubble wand in the dish, making sure that you coat it with plenty of solution, then blow bubbles!

4. To Wash: Rinse the bubble container with warm water and allow it to dry.

PARENTS: Bubble solution is not intended for human consumption.

Please be sure to supervise kids while playing with bubbles.

8. Natural Easy Peasy Playdough

Want playdough that lasts longer than store-bought?
This playdough is easy to make and store.
BONUS: Homemade playdough is non-toxic.
Takes less than 10 minutes to prepare, and kids will play for hours!

Materials:

1 cup All-purpose Flour
1 cup Water
2 teaspoons Cream of Tartar
⅓ CUP Table Salt (YES ⅓ CUP)
1 TBSP Vegetable or Canola oil
Gel food coloring

1. Mix flour, cream of tartar, and salt in a 2-quart saucepan.
2. Add a few drops of the food coloring into the water.
3. Stir colored water into the flour mixture and 1 Tablespoon of vegetable oil.
4. Heat your burner to medium/low heat, and stir. Cook and stir until the playdough begins to solidify. The lumps are OK.
5. Keep stirring until it starts to get solid. The lumps are OK.
6. NOTE: If your stove is already hot or you have a gas stove, this will only take 20-30 seconds. It may take 2-3 minutes if your electric stove needs to heat up.
7. Keep stirring!
8. The dough becomes thicker and a little lumpy. Keep stirring!
9. When the dough gathers around your spoon, you are done! 20 seconds or 2 minutes, depending on how hot your stove is.
10. Remove the play dough from the saucepan and put it on wax paper or a plate to cool.
11. Lumps? Squish and knead the dough once it's cooled.
12. Knead the dough for 1-2 minutes to get the lumps out and get the best consistency.
13. Store in a plastic bag or plastic container after each use.

NOTE: Make sure the dough is completely cooled so mold doesn't grow. 1 batch makes 2 cups. About 4 containers of store-bought playdough.
Tip: Make 4-6 batches while the pot is hot.
Tip: Half the recipe if you want to make different colors.
Tip: Purchase a large 2 lb. Pure Cream of Tartar on Amazon versus purchasing the little containers at the grocery store
Tip: Use GEL food coloring for vibrant colors that last a long time
Tip: Use the total amount of salt. Salt keeps the dough from sticking and helps preserve it.

9. Spider – Races

Materials:

Spider Rings (different colors are best, so you know teams)

Milkshake Straw

Directions:

1. Set the timer for 1-2 minutes

2. Determine the start and finish line.

3. The child must use the straw to blow the spider from start to finish line. Most times back and forth wins.

10. Witch Pitch

Materials:

Candy corn
Mini witch cauldrons or little buckets (bigger buckets for younger kids)

Directions:

1. Determine the start and finish lines

2. The child tosses candy corn into the witch's cauldrons/buckets. The most candy corn in the cauldrons/buckets wins.

3. Teams or individuals have 1-2 minutes to see how many candy corns they can make into the cauldrons/

11. The Jack Stack

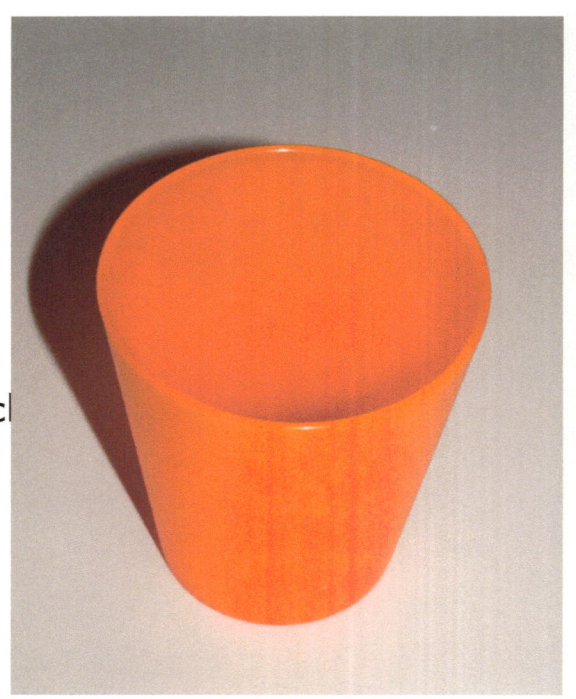

Materials:

Orange plastic cups
Black Sharpie marker

Directions:

Stack the cups into a pyramid shape. Use the blacl Sharpie to color on some cups to make them look like a pumpkin (eyes, nose, mouth, two stripes for the bottom of the pumpkin).

The child has 1-2 minutes to knock down the "pumpkin stack" and rebuild. Bonus points for restacking correctly in the shape of the pumpkin.

12. Big Pumpkin Kid Balloon Race

Materials:

2 XXL orange shirts
Black puffy fabric paint
Lots of balloons, filled and tied.

Directions:

1. Place a sheet of wax paper in between the shirt layers, so the paint doesn't leak through.
2. Draw a cute Jack-o-Lantern smiley face on the front of the shirts with the black puffy fabric paint. Silly faces are fun!
3. Let the paint dry for 1-2 hours. Overnight is best.

Fun family tradition to start this year.

The Party (Home or Classroom);
1. Ask two child volunteers who are OK with personal space invasion.
2. The child puts on the orange T-shirt.
3. Race to fill the shirt with balloons, turning the T-shirt into a giant pumpkin.
4. Sumo wrestling is fun. CAUTION. Warn children to only bump gently and ensure they are in an open area. No broken skulls allowed. BONUS: Easy to store the shirts year after year.

Top 11

Chapter Five

CREEPY CRAFTS

1. ORANGE FACE PUMPKINS

Ingredients:

1 Orange per person

1 Black Sharpie marker per person

Directions:

Draw a pumpkin face on your orange!

Voila! You now have a healthy snack for school AND adorable decorations for your home or classroom!

2. GUMMY WORM PUMPKINS

Ingredients:

Orange tissue paper   Gummy worms

Green tissue paper   Twist tie, yarn or jute

Directions:

1. Cut 8in x 8 in squares of orange tissue paper
2. Cut the length of the tissue paper into ½-inch long strips
3. Place approximately 5 gummy worms in the center of the orange tissue paper
4. Gather the orange tissue paper together in 1 hand and with the other hand tie together with a twist tie or yarn or jute.
5. Wrap the green tissue paper around the gathered orange to create the green stem of the pumpkin and close the pumpkin together.
6. Voila! Adorable pumpkins with a surprise inside!

40

3. CANDY CORN ROCKS

Directions:

1. Wash rocks with soap and water. Let it dry.
2. Cover the surface you will be painting on. Use a paper plate on a disposable table cloth for easy cleanup.
3. Paint the top - of the rock white.
4. Paint the middle - of the rock yellow.
5. Paint the bottom - of the rock orange.
6. Let completely dry
7. Draw cute faces on the candy corn rocks when done. (Or don't! Lol)

Materials:
Flat small rocks pointed at the top

Markers or paints (orange, yellow, white)
Cup of water for paints
Black Sharpie Pen

4. MONSTER ROCKS

Directions:

1. Wash rocks with soap and water. Let dry
2. Use a paper plate on a disposable tablecloth. Easy cleanup.
3. Paint the rock the solid color you want your monster.
4. Use a Sharpie marker to draw faces on your monster.
5. Optional: Glue on wiggly eyes, (faster and easier than painting eyes). Use Elmer's school glue with kids. Let Dry.
6. Give to friends and family. Decorate your walk to your house. Place on your favorite nature trail for decor.
Have FUN!!!

Materials:
Flat, disfigured shaped rocks
Markers, paints

Cup of water for paints.
Wiggly eyes, optional
Elmer's School Glue, optional

5. CHALKBOARD PUMPKINS

Materials:

Plastic pumpkin
Acrylic paint
Paintbrush
Sidewalk chalk

Mixing bowl
Craft stick
Baking soda
Water

Directions:

1. Make your own DIY chalkboard paint. Pour 2 oz of acrylic paint in a bowl. A glass bowl is best. Plastic bowls could stain.

2. Add 2 TBSP Baking soda. Mix well with the craft stick.

3. Paint the fake pumpkin with the paint mixture. Dry 1-2 hours. Paint a second coat. Dry 1-2 hours.

4. Your pumpkin is ready to be drawn on! Use sidewalk chalk to color and decorate your pumpkin!

Tips n Tricks:

1. Remember, chalkboards don't have to be black. Use ANY color of acrylic paint for your base.

2. If you want to erase any chalk drawings or mistakes, simply wet a paper towel and wash it off. Wait until the pumpkin is dry before creating again with the chalk.

3. Write messages on your chalkboard pumpkin.

6. KITTY HANDPRINT HALLOWEEN CARD OR POSTER

Materials:
Construction paper black, orange, and yellow
Paintbrush
Scissors
Glitter markers
Wiggly eyes
Washable paint
Pencil
School glue
Markers

Directions:

1. Fold the construction paper sheet in half, opening to the LEFT.

2. Paint hand. Stamp hand close to the top of the paper, fingers are facing upward. Dry for 1-2 hours.

3. Rotate the paper so the card now opens correctly to the right. The handprint should now be on the bottom, fingers facing down. (the legs of the cat)

4. Black construction paper. Use your pencil to sketch a circle and two triangles. Cut out the circle and two triangles for the kitty's face and ears.

5. Glue the face to the top of the handprint. Glue the ears on top of the face. (the thumb of the handprint is the kitty's tail)

6. Yellow construction paper. Use your pencil to sketch out a moon and stars. Cut out the moon and stars and glue them onto the sky.

7. Glue on wiggly eyes to the face.

8. Use a silver glitter marker to add a nose, whiskers, and small triangles in the ears.

9. Write Trick or Treat or a fun message with markers.

10. Give your homemade card to a friend, teacher, or family member.

43

7. WHITE PUMPKINS STACK

Materials:

3 Real or faux pumpkins
3 different sizes
White acrylic paint
Paint brush
Black Sharpie (or black acrylic paint)

Directions:

Draw faces or actual drawings on each pumpkin.

Write Trick or Treat on the middle pumpkin.

OR just keep plain white.

Stack the pumpkins on top of each other, or place them next to each other.

8. LAUNDRY JUG JACK-O-LANTERN

Upcycling for the Win!

Materials:

Old Tide Pods container
Black Sharpie pen
Battery-operated lights or candle

Directions:

1. Blow dry the label. Warm the label, and it peels off. (back up: Soak the empty laundry container in hot soapy water. Use a degreaser to scrub the label off)

2. Dry the container with a rag. Or just let it dry.

3. Decorate the dry orange container with the black sharpie. Draw a cute jack-o-lantern face.

4. Add lights or candles inside. Turn to the blink function for a full scary effect.

BONUSES

1. Use the green GAIN laundry detergent pod container and make Frankenstein!
2. Use the white fragrance-free laundry detergent pods container for a ghost!

9. SIDEWALK CHALK ART

Materials:

Colored sidewalk Chalk
Open space to color

Directions:

1. Find a flat, open surface to create your masterpiece. Driveways, sidewalks, or parks are the best.
2. Draw your heart out.

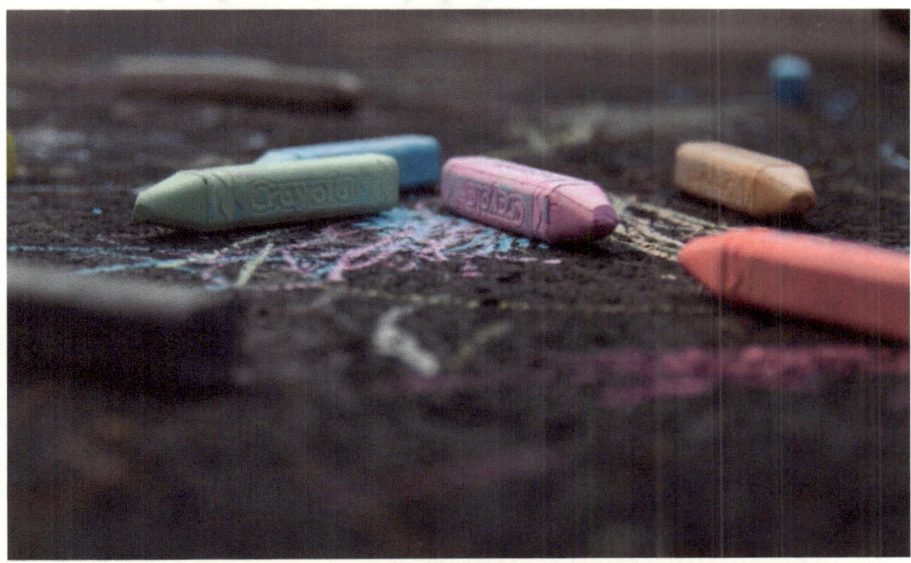

Ideas:
1. Have a friend or sibling lie down. Trace around their whole body. They can now stand up, and you can fill in the details. Maybe it's a crime scene, and someone just died, and you draw the evidence.
2. Create hopscotch, tic-tac-toe, obstacle course, Four Square, or whatever your imagination takes you!

10. SIDEWALK PAINTING

Materials:

Paintbrush
Cup or bucket of water

Directions:

1. Dip the paintbrush into the cup or bucket of water.
2. Start painting your masterpiece! Yes, with only water.
3. Take a picture of your masterpiece and send it to a Loved one.
4. Worry-Free! Mistakes dry up and disappear.

11. WHIP CREAM/SHAVING CREAM/ PUDDING ART

Materials:

13x9 pan

Whip Cream or pudding (edible art)

Shaving Cream (do NOT eat)

Directions:

1. Cover the cookie sheet or 13X9 pan with materials (whip cream, pudding, shaving cream)

2. Use your fingers to draw and create worlds and masterpieces. Explore the tactile world of writing your name, the ABCs, sight words, spelling words, and of course, Halloween words!

Finish the picture

Top 5

Chapter Six

EXTRAORDINARY EXTRAS

Top 5 Halloween Hacks for super busy mommas

1. Find local high schools

High school students are always looking for a way to do community service hours. One way to get hours in is to serve the community! Trunk-or-treat or a trick-or-treat at the high school. In Colorado, we have local high schools that go all out. Each activity and sports group decorate a part of the school hallway or classroom in a theme. Many offer games for the kids to play and, of course, hand out candy. Trunk-or-Treating can also be done in the parking lot, decorating trunks of cars or trucks, having games for the kids, and passing out candy. If your schools don't do this, suggest it to the PTO or school staff.

2. Find local churches

Churches love to fellowship. Find a local church that does a Trunk-or-Treat or a Fall activity in their social hall. These activities are a great way to meet new people and friends and have a safe environment for your kiddos to get some goodies.

3. Find local community opportunities.

Malls, businesses, organizations, etc., are always looking for ways to get their brand out there, and getting candy is a bonus.

4. Reuse. Recycle.

Remember that old costume you threw together a "few" years ago? Yeah! That one! Wear it again. If it doesn't fit anymore, that is what safety pins are for! Have your kids wear it or reuse parts.

5. Dollar Store Hacks!

Run to the dollar store and grab some party items. They seriously have the cheapest balloons! Grab some black balloons! You will be the hit!!!

BONUS HACK:

The day AFTER Halloween, be the first to run to the stores and grab their merchandise for a screaming deal for next year! Please share your fabulous finds with us and tag us @queenpublishingagency

We can't wait to see your finds and hacks!!!

Best Hacks

CONCLUSION

Holidays are fun, but boy, they can be stressful. It definitely can feel overwhelming, no matter how many kids you have. Some days you might feel like you are just barely surviving. And that's ok. There are different seasons of stress and activities going on.

Just remember, this is your child's holiday too. And sometimes, getting out of our stress and anxiety and focusing on making it a memorable holiday for our kids is all we busy mommas need for motivation. We included some coloring pages at the back of this book. You may print as many copies as you want and hand the kids some crayons, and it's just what "the doctor ordered" for you and the kids.

So relax.

You got this, momma.

You can do hard things!!!

Be sure to check out our other books

linktr.ee/ajkikumoto

Grab some freebies and sign up for our monthly newsletter
www.ajkikumoto.com

Enjoy!

If you found this book helpful, **please leave a favorable review on Amazon.com.** Simply go to Recent Purchases, scroll to the very bottom of where you purchased this book, and Click Leave a Review. We are forever grateful!

Bonus COLORING PAGES

for Busy Moms

Enjoy this free Coloring Page from AJKikumoto.com
More freebies available Linktr.ee/AJKikumoto

Enjoy this free Coloring Page from AJKikumoto.com
More freebies available Linktr.ee/AJKikumoto

Finish the picture

Enjoy this free Coloring Page from AJKikumoto.com
More freebies available Linktr.ee/AJKikumoto

RESOURCES

Dollar Tree Halloween Costumes - 8 Options Under $3! (2021, September 24). Passionate Penny Pincher. Retrieved 6 October 2022, from https://passionatepennypincher.com/5-easy-dollar-tree-halloween-costumes/?utm_source=dlvr.it&utm_medium=twitter&=1

Rodriguez, S. G. [thenovicehomesteader]. (2022). *Laundry Jug Jack-o-Lantern The Soccer Mom Blog the soccer mom blog.com. TikTok @ thenovicehomesteader.* TikTok.

Easy Homemade Vanilla Ice Cream. (2018, March 21). Allrecipes. Retrieved 6 October 2022, from https://www.allrecipes.com/recipe/63952/easy-homemade-vanilla-ice-cream/

4 Easy Ways to Make Ice Cream Without an Ice Cream Machine. (2020, September 3). Allrecipes. Retrieved 6 October 2022, from https://www.allrecipes.com/article/make-ice-cream-without-machine/

Build your own monster.

LilacsAndCharcoal - Etsy. (n.d.). *LilacsAndCharcoal.* Etsy. Retrieved 6 October 2022, from https://www.etsy.com/shop/LilacsAndCharcoal

Halloween Skulls.

Welch, L. (2021, July 15). *75 DIY Halloween Decorations You Can Make on the Cheap With Household Items.* Oprah Daily. Retrieved 6 October 2022, from https://www.oprahdaily.com/life/g28190402/diy-halloween-decorations/

2Halloween Monster Wreath. (2018, August 27). Kara Creates. Retrieved 6 October 2022, from https://karacreates.com/halloween-monster-wreath/

Minute to Win It Halloween Games. (2020, September 26). Happiness Is Homemade. Retrieved 6 October 2022, from https://www.happinessishomemade.net/halloween-minute-to-win-it-party-games/

Chalkboard Paint Pumpkin. (2022). Crayola.com. Retrieved 6 October 2022, from https://www.crayola.com/crafts/chalkboard-paint-pumpkin-craft/

Handprint Halloween Card. (2022). Crayola.com. Retrieved 6 October 2022, from https://www.crayola.com/crafts/chalkboard-paint-pumpkin-craft/

The Easiest Homemade Playdough Recipe {Lasts for Months!}. (2022, March 9). Living Well Mom. Retrieved 6 October 2022, from https://livingwellmom.com/easy-homemade-playdough-recipe/

Bloom, A. (n.d.). ***Big Pumpkin Kid Balloon Race.***

www.ingramcontent.com/pod-product-compliance
Lightning Source LLC
Chambersburg PA
CBHW041553120626
46551CB00002B/195